The Indo-Pacific Library

NORTH & SOUTH KOREA

TOWNLANDS PRIMARY SCHOOL
EARL SHILTON

Graham Houghton & Julia Wakefield

CONTENTS

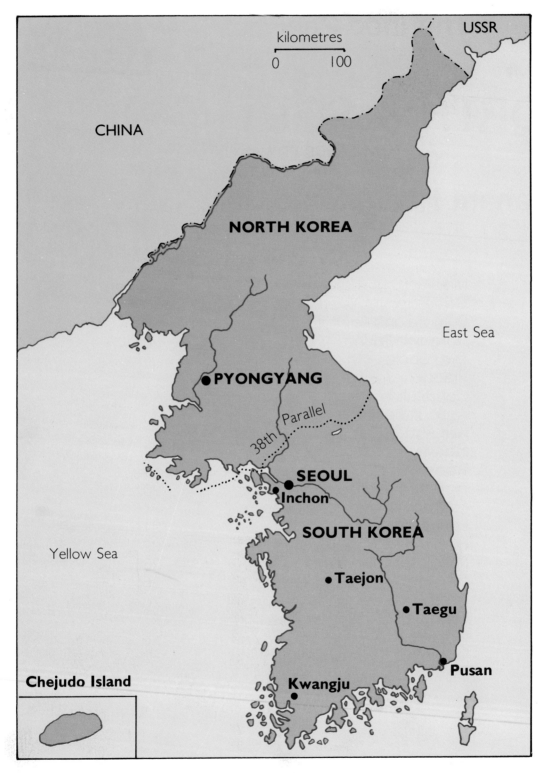

NORTH & SOUTH KOREA

Geography

Korea is a mountainous peninsula which extends southward from northern China into the Pacific Ocean. To the east lies Japan, and the north-eastern corner of Korea borders the USSR. It is about half the size of Japan. The peninsula is divided into communist North Korea and the Republic of Korea in the south.

Korea's hills and mountains cover nearly 80 per cent of the land. The lowest land is in the south and west, where the most fertile crops can be grown. The eastern coast consists of steep cliffs, while the western coast has winding rivers and mud flats. There are many small islands off this coast which are in fact ridges and mountains which have sunk into the sea, whereas the eastern side of Korea has been slowly tilting upwards over a period of millions of years.

Korea's major rivers flow west and south into the Yellow Sea and the Pacific Ocean. The eastern flowing rivers are short and fast flowing. The larger rivers are important for irrigating the rice fields. Dams have been built on several of them to control flooding and to serve hydro-electricity plants.

Climate and Rainfall

Korea has a temperate climate. It has hot, wet summers and cold, dry winters, but only in the far north are the winters bitterly cold. The hottest months, June, July, and August, are also the wettest months. Extremes in temperature and rainfall occur in different parts of Korea, because of the height of its mountains and the difference in latitude between North and South.

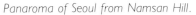
Panaroma of Seoul from Namsan Hill.

Natives of Korea: The Chital deer   *and the Tockay gecko.*

Flora and Fauna

There is a great variety of plant life in Korea, in keeping with its varied climate. There are alpine plants and pine trees in the North and in the mountainous regions, deciduous plants in the central western lowlands, and evergreen, 'warm/temperate' plants in the islands in the south and west.

    Animals found in highland Korea are similar to those found on Japan's Hokkaido Island, and in China and Siberia. Deer, brown bears, and the Manchurian weasel are examples. Tigers and lynx are found only in North Korea. In the lowlands black bears, river deer, and the Mandarin Vole are found. Leopards, wolves and wild boar are also natives of Korea. The native birds include the black grouse, the three-toed woodpecker, the hawk, owl and the ring-necked pheasant.

The People

The Korean people belong to the Altaic family of races, which includes the Turks and the Mongols. It is believed that the first inhabitants of Korea were hunter/gatherers who lived near the river banks and by the shore. They were pushed into poorer lands by farming peoples from the North. The Altaic migrants spread southwards and moved into Japan as well. Korea has been invaded many times by the Chinese, and the Japanese, but it has maintained a national identity since the seventh century A.D.

Language

The Korean language shares many characteristics with Manchurian and Mongolian. It is totally unlike Chinese. However, like the Japanese tongue, it has absorbed many Chinese words due to centuries of Chinese influence.

History

Ancient Chosŏn

Korea's people were at first a collection of scattered tribes, led by strong family groups called clans. Korea was first united in the North by a dynasty called Ancient Chosŏn which lasted for 1,200 years. Ancient Chosŏn was eventually conquered by the Han Empire of China in 109 B.C.

Chinese influence did not last long however, for there arose a number of powerful leagues in Korea who fought each other for the Kingdom. The three strongest leagues were the Koguryŏ, the Paekche, and the Silla. These were in continual conflict with each other for three hundred years, until Silla finally united the whole peninsula in 668 A.D.

Thousand year-old statues guard the Royal Silla tombs (below) at Kumgek.

The Silla

The three leagues made use of China's advanced learning during this period although they were by no means on peaceful terms with the Chinese. The Buddhist religion and Confucian philosophy were introduced from China between the fourth and sixth century A.D., and the Kingdoms were organised according to Confucian statecraft.

The people of Silla enjoyed peace and prosperity and many advances were made in learning and the arts. Wood block printing of Buddhist scriptures was widespread, and this brought literature to many people for the first time.

Koryo

Early in the tenth century A.D. the Silla government was overthrown and replaced by the Koryŏ Dynasty. The new Kingdom extended Korea's borders further north. In the eleventh century the Tripitaka was compiled, a huge library of Buddhist scriptures carved in wooden blocks. However, in 1126, the Koryŏ Palace was destroyed in a huge fire and many thousands of books were lost. It was after this disaster that the Koryŏ developed the world's first known moveable metal type.

Mongol Invasions

The Koryo's stability was rocked in the twelfth century by conflicts between the warrior and scholar classes. The Mongol Empire was forming in the north at this time and after a series of Mongol invasions the Koryŏ Court fled to Kanghwado Island. Another Tripitaka was carved on this island, which represented a declaration that Buddha would protect the Korean people from the Mongols.

The Chang Kyung Palace, royal residence until the 1800s.

Chosŏn

When the Mongol Empire came under China's control late in the fourteenth century, the Koryŏ attempted to reform its government. However, disputes were arising between the Buddhist and the Confucian scholars. The Confucians stressed the importance of family ties, and the power and extravagance of the Buddhist monasteries was heavily criticised. In 1392 the Yi Dynasty established the new Kingdom of Chosŏn. Confucianism was its creed, and Buddhism declined in importance. To spread the philosophy, Confucian literature was printed using the new metal type. Under King Sejong the Great (1418–1450), there were many advances in administration, science and medicine, the arts, and in the Korean language. Sejong was the creator of the Han-gŭl, a Korean alphabet, which replaced the Chinese characters that had been previously used. He also improved the lot of the peasant classes, introducing irrigation systems which controlled both droughts and floods, and he reformed the land tax system.

Main audience chamber,
Chang Duk Palace.

Japanese Invasion

In 1592 Korea was invaded by Japan when it refused to grant the Japanese army right of passage during its invasion of China. The war dragged on for five years until a second invasion in 1597. Many of Korea's craftsmen and scientists were taken to Japan, and much of their land was devastated by the war.

The Korean Renaissance

During the seventeenth and eighteenth centuries Korea became open to international trade and turned its back on the aristocracy's disdain for commerce and technology. There was a search for a fresher national identity, painters depicted the scenery of Korea rather than imitating the Chinese style. Maps were compiled using wood blocks, and many more books were printed, including books on Europe and Catholicism.

Catholic Persecution

Despite this new-found freedom of ideas, Catholics were severely persecuted in the nineteenth century. In 1864 a new boy-King ascended to the throne, under the control of his Regent, Taewon-gun. Taewon-gun violently opposed the infiltration of western ideas. He introduced further measures against the Catholics, which incited the French to attack Kanghwado Island. There followed several conflicts with European, Russian, and American ships which attempted to force Korea to re-open commercial relations, but Korea fiercely resisted them all. Finally, after Taewon-gun was overthrown in 1873, the Japanese attacked Pusan and Inchon, and Korea reluctantly agreed to sign a trade treaty with Japan in 1876. Similar treaties were signed with the United States, Great Britain, Germany, Russia, and France during the following decade.

Internal Conflict

There were many Koreans who disagreed violently with these treaties. A movement was formed called *Tonghak*, or 'Eastern Learning', which called for the equality of all people and rejected trade with Japan and the West. It was very popular with the farmers, who were being cruelly exploited by the Government, and it was only after a violent conflict followed by widespread executions that some compromises were made.

The Second Japanese Invasion

Once more torn apart by internal conflicts, Korea became vulnerable to foreign invasion. In 1894 the Japanese attacked China and helped to crush the Tonghak movement. After 1906 Japan took over Korea's government entirely.

The Koreans resisted fiercely, using guerilla tactics, while the Japanese attempted to destroy Korean national identity. Thousands of books on Korean history were destroyed. Korean newspapers were banned, and Korean children were not given the opportunity to learn to read or write.

An artists impression of The Sino-Japanese War 1894.

Declaration of Independence

After the onset of World War I, Korean resistance leaders saw a chance of succeeding in their struggle. They had to show the world how horrific their oppression was by the Japanese. A Declaration of Independence was drawn up and secretly circulated throughout the country. On 1 March 1919, the Declaration was read, and peaceful street demonstrations were staged nationwide. The Japanese were taken by surprise and reacted with violence, shooting into the crowds and arresting thousands of demonstrators. Although the world did not attempt to condemn Japan, the demonstration was an important event for Koreans as it showed that the national spirit was still alive.

Division

The struggle continued into the 1920s and 1930s. Korea was used as a base for Japan's proposed invasion of China, and Korea's industry was developed along military lines. Finally, after the Japanese

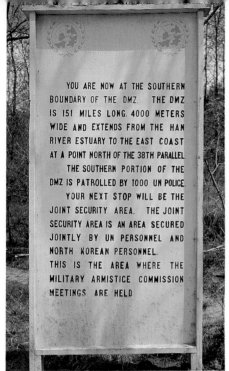

YOU ARE NOW AT THE SOUTHERN
BOUNDARY OF THE DMZ. THE DMZ
IS 151 MILES LONG. 4000 METERS
WIDE AND EXTENDS FROM THE HAN
RIVER ESTUARY TO THE EAST COAST
AT A POINT NORTH OF THE 38TH PARALLEL.
THE SOUTHERN PORTION OF THE
DMZ IS PATROLLED BY 1000 UN POLICE.
YOUR NEXT STOP WILL BE THE
JOINT SECURITY AREA. THE JOINT
SECURITY AREA IS AN AREA SECURED
JOINTLY BY UN PERSONNEL AND
NORTH KOREAN PERSONNEL.
THIS IS THE AREA WHERE THE
MILITARY ARMISTICE COMMISSION
MEETINGS ARE HELD

Explanatory sign. Southern boundary. DMZ.

The meeting hall in the De Military Zone — where North (in green) meets South (in grey).

surrender in 1945, Korea was divided between the United States of America and the Soviet Union. Two opposing Governments were established, which resulted in rigid regimentation in the North, and internal disorder in the South. In 1948 the Government of the Republic of Korea took over in the South from the United States military government.

The Korean War

On 25 June 1950, the North Koreans invaded South Korea, and within a month they had taken over. The United States Army retaliated, followed by troops from fifteen other nations, attempting to force the Communist troops back up to latitude 38° North. Just as it seemed as though this would be achieved, more Chinese troops invaded and Seoul fell once more to the Communists in January 1951. After the United Nations forces had taken Seoul on 12 March, the Russians called for a truce, and peace talks continued for two years until the ceasefire agreement was reached on 27 July 1953. The war was as devastating to the Korean economy as the Japanese occupation had been to the Korean culture.

The Third Republic

During the next eight years there was constant political strife between the old authoritarian and the new democratic parties. In 1961 there was a military coup staged by the Revolutionary Committee, which made way for the Third Republic in 1963, headed by President Park Chung Hee, and the nation began to achieve economic stability. Peaceful relations between North and South were restored in 1971.

The heart of modern Seoul.

On 26 October 1979, President Park Chung Hee was assassinated. Once more, Korea became divided politically and suffered economically, but it was saved from disaster by General Chun Doo Hwan, who was elected President of the Republic in 1980.

Modern Korea Under President Chun, North/South relations were restored and diplomatic ties with the Pacific Nations were greatly strengthened. Despite a North Korean attempt to assassinate President Chun while he was visiting Burma in October 1983, these relations have continued to improve. North Korea is now being pressured to come to an amicable agreement over the division of the Nation. An historic occasion occurred in September 1984 when President Chun visited Japan, and received an apology from Emperor Hirohito for the Japanese occupation. President Chun also makes regular visits to the United States, and many world leaders visit Seoul in their turn.

Constitution

South Korea South Korea's Constitution is led by a President elected by the 5,000 members of an electoral college, who are in turn elected by the people. The President's term of office is seven years, and he

The Capitol building, Seoul.

may not renew his office for a second term. The President presides over the State Council, and Cabinet, and is also Commander in Chief of the armed forces. He is entitled to appoint and to dismiss the Prime Minister and Cabinet Ministers as well as the senior public officials. In 1987 this Constitution was under review after mass riots. Under the State Council is the National Assembly, which consists of two hundred members, or more. They are elected by popular vote for a term of four years.

North Korea   North Korea's Constitution dates from 1972. The Supreme People's Assembly is elected by popular vote every four years. The Government is called the Administration Council and it is directed by the Central People's Committee. The Central Committee is elected by the Korean Worker's Party. Local Government is administered by People's Assemblies, which represent each city or province.

Agriculture

South Korea

In the last twenty years the number of people employed in South Korea's industry has grown from 8.7 per cent to 24.2 per cent. In contrast the number of agricultural workers has dropped from 63.1 per cent to 27.1 per cent; despite this, agricultural production doubled between 1962 and 1976 due to improved efficiency and farming methods. Since then growth has been slower, but Korea remains self-sufficient in the production of rice, its staple food crop.

Less than 25 per cent of South Korea's land can be cultivated, and even less is available in North Korea. New farming methods have concentrated on producing maximum yields, so high-yield varieties of rice and other crops have been introduced. Irrigation, fed by damming rivers and pumping up ground-water, is an important part of South Korea's modern agricultural method.

In addition to rice, a great variety of fruits and vegetables are produced in much greater quantities than twenty years ago. Examples are apples, tangerines, grapes, pears, peaches, and persimmons. The main reason for the rapid increase in fruit and vegetable growing is the introduction of plastic greenhouses.

Barley is becoming the second most important cereal crop, as it can be grown in the winter on the rice fields.

Livestock have increased dramatically in recent years, and consist of pigs, cattle, chickens, goats, and rabbits. Silk, an agricultural product which was once very important, has seriously declined in its importance in the last ten years, due to adverse trends in international trade.

A typical Korean village house.

Rice is planted in every available space.

North Korea

In 1982, 38 per cent of North Korea's population were still employed on the land. Nearly all the land is farmed by worker's co-operatives, and the rest belongs to the State. No one has the right to own land. The North Koreans have also concentrated on intense mechanisation and high yielding crops. Rice and potatoes are staple products; pigs and cattle are the most important forms of livestock.

Forestry

South Korea is regarded as a model for re-afforestation in the developing world. Whereas fifteen years ago South Korea's forests had been virtually destroyed, now 67 per cent of the land area is reserved for the production of timber. Forestry also remains an important industry in North Korea.

Fisheries

Fishing is another industry which has improved enormously in recent years in North and South Korea. Sailing and rowing boats were replaced by large motorised vessels and deep-sea fishing has become a major industry. The eastern coasts are among the best fishing grounds in the world.

Forestry workers tend tomorrow's timber.

Natural Resources

Energy

South Korea has very few sources of energy, and so has to import 75 per cent of its fuel, mostly in the form of crude oil. Other energy is supplied from nuclear power, and coal, whilst four per cent is produced by hydro-electric schemes. Most of South Korea's coal supplies have been exhausted, and its sources of natural gas have yet to be properly explored. The South Koreans are now exploring their surrounding seas for oil deposits. The North Koreans have had oil wells for thirty years, and also have an oil pipeline running from China.

Industry

Minerals

South Korea has a variety of mineral deposits, but mining is not a large industry. Iron ore, tungsten, silver, kaolin, limestone, lead ore, and zinc ore are all mined. North Korea has much greater mineral reserves, adding to those of South Korea nickel, manganese, and graphite.

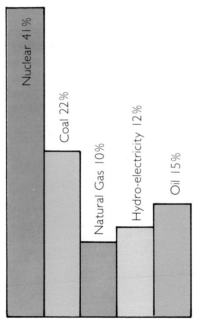

South Korea's projected energy sources for 1991

South Korean Industry

In the past twenty years South Korean industry has been completely revolutionised. The main key to South Korea's impressive industrial growth is its concentration on the export of manufactured goods. It

Copper processing one of Korea's growing industries.

has had to rely on trade, because it is so poor in natural resources.

The first growth industries were light ones such as textiles, but now half the manufactured goods in South Korea are products of the heavy engineering and chemical industries. In 1984 South Korea was the tenth largest steel producer in the world. Shipbuilding also became a very important industry. Other products of heavy industry are power plant equipment, and construction machinery.

Another vital industry is electronics. Televisions, stereos, tape-recorders, radios, electronic watches, video machines, calculators, micro-wave ovens, and small computers are the major products, three-fifths of which are exported. The motor industry is also expanding rapidly. To meet the energy demands of these industries, South Korea has oil refineries and two large petro-chemical complexes but still needs to import 75 per cent of its industrial fuel.

North Korean Industry

North Korea is also a large steel manufacturer and shipbuilder. Other products include textiles, pig-iron, copper, cement, and chemical fertilisers.

Trade and Commerce

South Korea
Exports in 1984 totalled 95 per cent of manufactured goods. Major items were steel, non-ferrous metals, industrial machinery, ships, automobiles, electronic goods, textiles, footwear, plywood, auto tyres, and plastic products.

In the same year oil made up nearly twenty per cent of total imports. Other imports include grain and other raw materials for manufacturing goods.

In the early years of its economic recovery half of South Korea's exports and more than three-quarters of its imports were taken over by the United States of America, and Japan. They are still important trading partners, but they now supply less than half of her imports. Europe and other Asian countries are becoming more important as trading partners.

North Korea
59 per cent of North Korea's exports are manufactured goods. Metal ores and their products are also very important. The chief imports are machinery and petroleum products. Half of North Korea's trade in 1981 was with communist countries, compared with 85 per cent 10 years earlier.

Imports

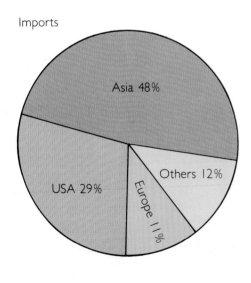

Exports

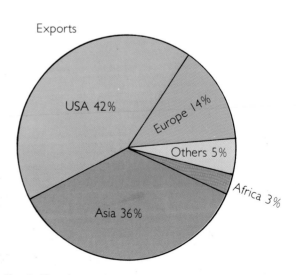

Imports and Exports (South Korea)

Transport and Communication

Railways and Roads   South Korea has improved its transport system at a record pace in the last few years. There is an efficient national railway system and Seoul has a subway system which totals more than 100 kilometres in length. There are new expressways connecting industrial areas to urban centres and linking mountainous areas with the coast.

North Korea's railway system is also very important for its industries.

Airports   There are many inland airports, and, from South Korea, international flights connect with six Japanese cities as well as five destinations in the United States. In addition there are flights to many cities in South East Asia, the Middle East, and Europe. South Korea also has twenty-one trading ports of which the largest is Pusan.

International flights in North Korea are limited to Moscow and Peking. The three main shipping ports are Chongjin, Hungnam, and Nampo near Pyonyang.

Communication   South Korea publishes 32 daily newspapers, and more than 1,700 periodicals. In contrast North Korea has only one official newspaper with a circulation of about one million.

South Korea has its own broadcasting systems for both radio and television, and a well-managed telephone system with satellite links to all parts of the world.

A crowded downtown Seoul street.

Main towns and Population

South Korea

Twenty per cent of South Korea's population live in the capital, Seoul, which supports nearly nine million people. Seoul is the administrative and business centre for South Korea and has been a city for 600 years. As it is only 40 Km. from the thirty-eighth parallel, security is very important with constant danger of attack from the North, despite the 1000 United Nations police in the De-Militiarised Zone (DMZ). (See Fig. 8a.)

North Korea

The capital of North Korea is Pyongyang, which was established in the 1950s. Its population is about one million and, in contrast to crowded Seoul, it is very spacious with many public parks.

Education

South Korea

The first six years of primary education are free for all South Korean children. After that follows three years of middle school, only free for students living in remote areas. Nearly 90 per cent of children go on to three years of high school, which can be either general, or vocational (leading to a trade qualification). Almost half the students enter vocational high schools.

Over 400 universities, colleges, and teachers' colleges offer courses lasting two to four years to higher students. There are also more than 100 post-graduate colleges. Although further education is expensive, most families regard it as necessary.

North Korea

In North Korea all schools have a technical emphasis, and manual labour is a compulsory part of education. Education is free and compulsory between the ages of seven and sixteen. Undergraduate university courses last between four and six years.

South Korean school girls visit Chang Duk Palace.

Health and Welfare

South Korea's rapid industrial development has resulted in a population explosion in the cities, as workers have come in from country areas. There is now a chronic housing shortage, made worse by the fact that property prices have become inflated far beyond the financial means of many people. Public housing schemes are being developed to help alleviate this problem.

Doctors' fees in South Korea are usually high and a medical insurance programme was recently introduced. By contrast, North Korea's State medical system provides free health care for everyone. There are not such acute housing problems in North Korea as the city populations are much smaller and the rents are usually low.

Wash days, Korean style.

Employment in cities often means crowded, poor housing conditions.

Religion and Festivals

Korea's oldest religion is Shamanism, the worship of spirits in natural objects. This is sometimes called animism. The Shamans were the priests of this religion. Animism is still practised in many rural areas.

Buddhism and Confucianism

Buddhism and Confucianism have been the dominant religions in Korea since its unification in 668 A.D. There are over seven and a half million Buddhists in South Korea and less than a million followers of Confucius; but Confucianism is more a philosophy and way of life than a religion, and it still has a strong influence on Korean society. It emphasises the importance of the family and the duty of children to respect their elders, particularly the father.

Golden Buddhas in Pulkuksa Temple, Pusan.

Christianity

There are one and a half million Catholics and over five million Protestants in South Korea. Christianity was revived in Korea in the twentieth century by leaders of the Resistance against the Japanese.

Others

Islam was introduced to Korea by Turkish soldiers fighting with the United Nation's forces during the Korean War. There are also a number of native religious movements which originated in the late nineteenth century, and called for social reform. Tonghak, the rural movement which was quelled by the Japanese, still survives under the name of Chŏngdogyo.

Festivals

Some of Korea's most important days are Independence Day on 1 March, Liberation Day which celebrates the surrender of the Japanese forces to the allies on 15 August 1945, and Ch'usok, Korean Thanksgiving Day. This is the great national holiday of the year, when people visit family tombs and make food offerings to their ancestors. There is a holiday devoted to the founder of Ancient Choson. Korean Alphabet Day celebrates the introduction of Han-gul, which is Korea's national written script. Also numerous folk festivals take place in many parts of Korea every year.

Christmas and New Year's Day are celebrated, as well as Folklore Day which is New Year's Day on the lunar calendar followed by the Buddhists.

The important national religious festival is Buddha's Birthday, or The Feast of Lanterns as it is also known.

Dancers of Pusan in colourful dress on Folklore Day.

The Arts

There has always been a lively tradition of painting and calligraphy in Korea, using Chinese techniques but in a style that is unique to Korea. Sculpture had its heyday when Buddhism was at its most powerful under the Chosŏn Kingdom. Korean architecture has similarities to that of both China and Japan, except the roofs of the pagodas curve upwards at the corners.

Korea's most famous craft is ceramic ware, particularly the Celadon of the Koryŏ Period. Korean potters were kidnapped by the Japanese in the sixteenth century and started the Japanese ceramics tradition.

Literature and Music Korea has a rich literary history, although it was greatly influenced by China. A popular form of poetry is the *Shijo*, which is always sung or chanted. Music is an essential part of the Korean way of life and takes many forms. There is Confucian ritual music, court music, Buddhist chants, and folk music. Vocal music tends to be accompanied by the beat of a drum only. In folk music, metal drums, gongs, and a type of oboe produce loud, fast rhythms to accompany dances. Western music has been popular for many years and South Korea has several symphony orchestras.

Music is vital to the Korean people.

Traditional national Korean dancers.

Traditional Korean architecture shows Chinese and Japanese elements. Changduk Palace, Seoul.

Sport and Recreation

South Korea has been selected to host the 1988 summer Olympics, and in 1986 it was host to the Asian Games. It is the second Asian country to be selected to host the Olympics (Japan was the first).

There are many western sports that have a following in Korea. They include soccer, baseball, volleyball, and basketball. Ancient sports which are now going through a popular revival include archery, *ssirum* (a form of wrestling), and *Tae Kwon Do*, a martial art which has become popular all over the world.

Korea also has a number of traditional games such as *Yut*, which is played during the New Year Holiday. It is a game of chance played with counters and four sticks which are thrown into the air, and serve in the same way as dice in western games. There are board games such as *Paduk* (called *Go*, in Japan), and *Changgi*, a type of chess. On lunar New Year's Day, the girls play see-saw, but with a difference. They jump onto the board in turn sending their partner high into the air. Swinging in a standing position is another game associated with the lunar New Year, and later in the month kite flying is popular.

Yuoido Plaza, Seoul, on Sunday.

Food and Clothing

Food

In Korea, the whole meal is served at the same time, rather than as separate courses. Rice is always the main dish. There are side dishes such as bean paste soup, roast beef and fish, accompanied by vegetables and seasoned with soy sauce, ginger, sesame seeds, ginseng and garlic. There are traditional feast days associated with a man's first and sixtieth birthdays.

Clothing

Western clothing is the norm in Korea now, although many women still wear the traditional flared blouse and long high-waisted skirt.

Ginseng roots drying. Ginseng is a health herb often thought to have magical properties.

Gazetteer: North Korea

Official name: Chosun Minchu-chui Inmin Konghwa-guk

Constitution: Communist

Head of State: Marshal Kim Il Sung

Head of Government: The Prime Minister, Kang Song San (1985)

Capital city: Pyongyang

Official language: Korean (North and South)

Area: 122,098 sq. km.

Population: 19.32 million (1984)

Climate: A warm temperature climate with very cold winters in the north.
Temperatures for Pyongyang: Jan. -7.8°C, July 24°C. Rainfall: 916 mm.

Weights and Measures: The metric system is in use alongside local
measurements

Currency: The *won* is the unit of currency in both North and South Korea

Religion: Buddhism is the main religion in both North and South Korea. There
are large minorities of Christians in both countries.

Airports and Shipping: The main airport is at Pyongyang. There are regular
flights to Moscow and Peking
The main ports are Chongjin, Hungnam, and Nampo for Pyongyang

Agricultural production: Rice and potatoes are the main crops.
Pigs are the main livestock.

Main exports: Metal ores,' and metal products

Main imports: Industrial machinery, petroleum

Main trading partners: China, USSR

North Korea's Flag: Horizontal stripes of blue, white, red, white, blue. In the
centre is a white circle containing a star.

North Korea's National Anthem: 'Shine bright, o dawn, on this land so fair' (*A
chi mun bin na ra i gang san*).

Gazetteer: South Korea

Official name: Han Kook

Constitution: Democratic Republic

Head of State: General Chun Doo-Hwan

Head of Government: The Prime Minister, Lho Shin Yong (1986).

Capital city: Seoul

Area: 98,992 sq. km.

Population: 40,430,137 (1984).

Highest mountain: Mount Paektusan (2,744 m)

Longest river: Amnokkang River (790 km)

Climate: There are warm summers and cold winters.
Temperatures for Seoul: Jan. -5°C, July 25°C. Rainfall: 1,250 mm.

Weights and Measures: The metric system is used

Airports and Shipping: Korean Air Lines is the national carrier and flies
regularly to a number of overseas destinations. Kimpo International Airport at
Seoul is the main airport. Pusan is the main shipping port.

Agricultural production: The main crops are rice and other cereals, and
tobacco

Main exports: Consumer goods, ships

Main imports: Industrial raw materials

Main trading partners: USA, Japan

South Korea's Flag: The flag is called T'aegukki. It is white with the Yin-Yang
symbol in the centre. Four black symbols, one in each corner represent
Heaven, Earth, Fire, and Water.

The National Anthem: 'God watch o'er our land forever'

Index